THE GOOD NO

THE GOOD NO

How to Stop Overcommitting,
Avoid Burnout, and
Maintain Strong Relationships

DAVID WARREN

The Good No

Copyright © 2025 David Warren

All rights reserved.

ISBN: 979-8-9924769-0-3 (paperback)

ISBN: 979-8-9924769-1-0 (ebook)

Edited by Erica Ellis.

Cover design by Kostis Pavlou.

An Oomiyasa publication.

www.thegoodnobook.com

For Shelby and Adelaide

Contents

Preface 9

To Decline Is Human 15

Good No Guiding Principles 27

The Roles 31

How Am I Supposed to Remember All These Dang Roles? 61

Bullies, Bias, and Bullshit 63

How Much Time Do You Have Anyway 65

Summary 69

Acknowledgments 71

Preface

Call it luck or corporate divinity, but in every job I've had, I found myself working alongside or managing what must be an above-average number of uniquely talented, whip-smart, creative, collaborative, good-natured people. Truly superstars. They are the up-and-coming, high-potential folks who consistently nail the deliverable, dazzle the client, double their quota, save the day, stick the landing, rock the casbah, etc. You may know the type. You might *be* the type.

These are the folks that managers fight to get staffed on their projects. New hires emulate them. Customers fall in love with them. Their peers revere them while their insides burn with jealousy. They win the awards for "Most Dependable," "Employee of the Quarter," "Manager of the Year," and "Most Cloneable." Their careers and reputations grow steadily (as do their bosses') because they are always willing to go above and beyond, do whatever it takes, burn the midnight oil, take it on the chin, and "play hurt" if they get sick.

These are also the people at the highest risk of going from burning brightest to burning out. Why? For the same reasons that put them in high demand in the first place. Star managers want star players on their projects. If they can't get them full time, they'll take them part time. If they can't get them part time, they'll take what they can, even if it's just a few extra hours. Or it may be a one-off request to sit in on one meeting "just to be a fly on the wall and offer a few thoughts."

A few days later, they're asked, "Could you give this fifty-slide presentation a quick read and add some thoughts?"

And then a few days after that, "Would you sit in on this interview and complete this scorecard to help us evaluate this candidate's fit?"

And then a day later, "Can you join our little ideation 'sesh' about the new product features?"

And the next day, "I recommended you to serve on the offsite advisory committee."

And the next day, "Would you be willing to be a coach to this new hire?"

And a few hours later, "I know this isn't something you normally do, but can you sit in and cover me on the weekly update meeting?"

And, and, and…

Over a year, these little investments can add up to days and weeks carved out from day-to-day work time. And if there isn't day-to-day work time to spare, then it gets carved out from the time that would otherwise be spent on things like exercising, picking up the dry cleaning, mowing the yard, going on a date, learning the bassoon, attending kids' school plays, weekends, vacations, eating, and sleeping. In a word, ***life***. They find themselves stuck in a riptide of obligations from which they can't swim free, and they start to drown.

When this would happen to someone on my team, I would receive an urgent request for a private conversation. They would share how overwhelmed they were with all the additional work they were taking on and the uncertainty they felt about their ability to continue at the pace they were running. Their confidence was down. Some were stressed to the point of illness and on the verge of quitting. It would be difficult to hear this from anyone with whom I had an informal coaching relationship, but it was more painful and personal if it came from someone who worked for me, as it suggested that I might be part of the problem. When I asked these smart, capable, resourceful professionals why they were taking on more than they could handle, I would hear one of two replies:

"Well, it's not like I *can* say no."
Or…"I don't know *how* to say no."

So we'd talk through options to help them negotiate a deadline extension or reprioritize a few activities. Things would be better for a few weeks or months. But very often, the stream of requests for time and effort would return and be granted, the workload would spike, the feelings of frustration and helplessness would return, and they would quit, leaving the company, the team, and me down yet another superstar.

This situation is not uncommon. Every people-leader has "the superstar that got away" stories. And it's not just the fresh-faced, new-to-the-work-world individual contributors who experience this fate. It happens to managers, executives, and even senior executives who are widely respected, deeply trusted, and highly valued (and highly compensated). Despite all the trappings and resources that come with professional success, they also struggle with saying no.

People working part time or full time for an hourly wage can be even more susceptible to being stuck in this situation. These jobs often offer less protections for employees. Saying no could be used by a manager as a reason for not getting staffed on a shift or approved for overtime, or even for getting fired.[1]

Most people are self-aware about their situation. Whether they believe they can't say no or don't know how to say

---

1   Check out the *Reddit* subgroup r/antiwork for some depressing examples of this.

no, they *know* that at least part of the problem is on them. Sometimes, they can even articulate why they struggle with saying no.

I'm bad at setting boundaries.
I've said yes to this in the past. It would be weird to say no.
If I don't do it, no one else will.
If I let someone else do this, it won't be done right.
I don't want to upset anyone.
I didn't get to where I am today by telling people I won't do something.
What the hell else am I supposed to say?

So they say yes. Over and over. They burn out. Then they leave.

This book started as a workshop that I developed off to the side of my desk after having another conversation with a stressed-out superstar who I suspected would be heading for the exit soon unless something changed. I put together a few negotiation and facilitation techniques I picked up in my career, from my early days as an hourly employee, a union member, and an independent contractor up to my time in the corporate world. These techniques helped me improve the quality of my work life but, more importantly, they helped me create and protect space for my personal life.

I called the workshop the "Good No" on the calendar invite. Attendance was optional. Three dozen people showed up. I did an informal thirty-minute presentation and invited volunteers to try out some of the techniques in a role play. While the methods weren't difficult to understand, I was still surprised at how quickly and easily people could apply them to the mocked-up scenarios. I made some tweaks and did another workshop. Weeks and months later, I heard people sharing "good no" examples they used. Since then, I've delivered the workshop many more times in various formats, iterating on the content along the way. I kept getting requests to share the presentation from people I didn't know who had heard about it from former teammates, so I ultimately decided to package everything here.

This book is not a "do less, get paid more" how-to manual for people trying to game the system, shirk their responsibilities, and move their careers forward. This book is for people who understand that success and advancement often mean saying yes to things outside their job description. At the same time, they are at a place where they can't maintain the effort or energy required to deliver the great work that earned them the respect of their bosses and coworkers. And worse, it may be interfering with their ability to maintain and enjoy relationships outside of work. If this feels familiar, I hope the following pages will help you gain some time, energy, and joy.

Let's get into it, shall we?

To Decline Is Human

Have you ever been in the presence of a three-year-old for an extended period of time? If so, you may have witnessed a scenario where a hapless parent tries to convince their child to do something but finds themselves receiving a stream of refusals.

"Come to the table."
"No."
"Keep your shoes on."
"NO!"
"Eat your peas."
"Nonononononono."
"Take those peas out of your nose."
"NoooooOOOOOOOOooo!"
"Let's go put your pajamas on."
"No. No! NO!"

These moments are incredibly trying for parents (but super funny when you're *not* the parent). This behavior is not a sign of a spoiled or "difficult" child. In fact, it's a normal part of childhood development. There's even a term for it. "Toddler refusal." Saying no is how children begin to explore and exercise their free will. They learn that "no" is a powerfully efficient word to express their feelings or establish their point of view. It is a demonstration of control, confidence, and independence.[2]

All of us drove our parents and babysitters nuts at one time with such behavior. But then what happened? As we aged, we became more agreeable (most of us anyway, and not all the time) thanks to the adults in our lives, who taught us that saying no can be disrespectful or "bad." Over time, we became socially conditioned to avoid upsetting others and limiting our "nos" to only those moments deemed "appropriate." Saying yes and being obedient was the mark of a good child and earned us praise and awards. We collected stars and stickers on classroom whiteboards, high grades for comportment on our report cards, and glowing reviews shared during parent-teacher conferences. For the first decade of our lives, the grown-ups created thousands of moments like these to reinforce acceptable and compliant behavior.

As we passed through adolescence and entered our teenage years, we chose where we would sit on the rebellion spectrum. We became hyper-aware of how our peers responded to rules and directions and how their behavior impacted their status with adults and peers. Some of us

---

[2] S. A. Denham, S. A., *Emotional Development in Young Children.* (Guilford Press, 1998).

rebelled outwardly by arguing with figures of authority, flouting school dress codes, or blaring death metal music from car stereos with the windows open. Meanwhile, the rest did their best to meet the expectations of their parents, grandparents, uncles, teachers, rabbis, priests, coaches, bosses, parents of friends, and everyone else who had a perspective on good choices to make. Here are a few from the *Greatest Hits* collection:

Well, what did the teacher say you should do?
Listen to me, okay? I'm a lot older than you.
Do what the coach tells you.
You might want to take the path of least resistance and just give in.
When the boss says jump, you ask, "How high?" Got it?
Don't think. Just do.
Is that what [insert name of relevant religious figure or annoying goody-two-shoes kid in school] would do?

Triggered yet?

GenX-ers in the U.S. will remember the "Just Say No to Drugs" campaign during the eighties. While the intention to protect kids from harming themselves was right, the guidance was laughable because it didn't include any helpful techniques or language that kids could apply in those situations. *Just say no?* To the peers whose opinion of you determines where you get to play in the complex social hierarchy of teendom? That's the advice? Seriously? Brilliant. Thanks.

Finally, we entered the adult world. We landed jobs where status and hierarchy are determined by experience, tenure, performance, politics, and, occasionally, a teench of nepotism. Those of us with ambition and goals quickly learned valuable lessons about the benefits of saying yes. In order to move up in salary and position, you were well served by coming across as being capable, agreeable, and collaborative to managers, coworkers, and customers. The gold stars and stickers with our names written on them morphed into raises, bonuses, promotions, team meeting shout-outs, parking spaces, "President's Club" vacations, and stock options. We learned that saying yes to extra shifts, Friday evening conference calls, and stretch assignments earned respect and kudos. Saying no was viewed as damaging to collaboration, camaraderie, and the "one team" culture.

Have you ever been to a team meeting or a conference call where the leader is praising a colleague for giving up personal time, denying sleep, shunning food, and waving off emergency medical care to get a shipment out or a deal done? We respond with kudos, applause, and "flexing bicep" emojis to acknowledge the superhuman will and dedication of colleagues whose bodies and brains know no limits. Nothing better than being recognized as a "go-to" person, right? Right?

It *is* good to be well-regarded and respected at work. Saying yes to complicated and time-consuming tasks is a great way to learn new things, develop skills, advance one's career, and demonstrate good character. Saying yes is *usually* the correct answer, but not always.

Ask a high achiever what is the secret to their success, and they will often say something about the effect of hard work, focus, and discipline. Trite but true. Unless you are a savant with rare genetic gifts for processing information and converting it into something of value, high achievement requires something else. Time, which, to quote another trite but true adage, is one's most valuable resource. When we commit to something that we genuinely do not have time for, even though it may contribute to our professional success, a whole host of emotions can get triggered:

- Anxiety about the ability to complete a task on time.
- Resentment towards the person who asked/demanded that you take on extra work.
- Disappointment towards the company because there aren't more resources available.
- Anger that you were deceived into believing that the request was simpler than it actually was.
- Shame that you weren't able to advocate for yourself more effectively.
- Helplessness in an environment where others have more control over your to-do list than you do.

- Disengagement from a culture that feels like it puts a disproportionate value on *what* gets done rather than *how*.

These feelings that stem from overcommitment are indicators of what I'll call a Bad Yes. While these emotions often hit us after the fact, sometimes we experience them in the moment while saying yes, even though we know we shouldn't—or can't!

Bad Yesses aren't rare. We offer them up all the time for reasons mentioned earlier (respect, rewards, advancement, etc.). An occasional Bad Yes may cause some temporary disruption. It's similar to getting a sore back that takes a few hours to work itself out after sitting in a car during a long road trip. But a string of Bad Yesses can create more serious long-term conditions affecting our mood, sleep, performance, and health. Now that sore back is akin to the experience of some long-haul truckers who spend years of their lives in a sitting position and suffer from chronic pain, obesity, and heart conditions.

Let's assume you know all this already. You have delivered hundreds of Bad Yesses in your life to coworkers, friends, significant others, family, and even strangers. You know they are bad. Let's also assume that you are a super self-aware person who can recognize when a Bad Yes might be about to slip out of your mouth, and in those moments, you commit every synapse in your brain to resist the temptation. And yet, you…still…say…(GAH)…yes.

Why?

There are many reasons, and rarely do they include temporary insanity. Maybe you don't like confrontation. Or perhaps you can't stand the idea of offending someone or hurting their feelings by turning them down. Maybe you suffer from relationship karma FOMO and can't stand missing an opportunity to build a closer bond with your "Requester." Are you not eating and sleeping well? Fatigue and hunger[3] can affect your energy levels and leave you feeling less willing to negotiate.

Maybe it's not you. Sometimes, Requesters are better at requesting than you are at refusing. This is especially true when someone appeals to your ego. A Requester might say something like, "Oh, but you're *so good* at this." Well, yes, that may very well be true. You're probably good at lots of things. You might be great at carving 3D portraits of people's faces out of cantaloupes. That doesn't mean you should have to serve as the company cantaloupe caricaturist for the next offsite.

> **"It's only by saying 'no' that you can concentrate on the things that are really important."**
> **–Steve Jobs**

---

3   Emily Zitek and Jordan Alexander, "I Need Food and I Deserve a Raise: People Feel More Entitled When Hungry," *Academy of Management Proceedings* 2014, no.1 (2014): 14357.

Well said. Of course, this quote would land better if Steve Jobs hadn't been known for never accepting any response from his team except yes. But the thinking is correct, assuming the word "things" includes the stuff outside of work mentioned earlier: family and friends. Physical and mental health. Exercise. Natural light. Sleep. Nutrition. And yes, work. In order to protect your time and give the proper amount of attention to these things, you must learn to deliver a Good No.

What is a Good No? Well, it can sound very different depending on the situation, the personality of the Requester, and their relationship to you. Essentially, it is a negotiation technique that accomplishes two objectives:

1. Preserve your ability to focus your energy and effort on essential things.
2. Maintain or build credibility, trust, and respect with others, especially the Requester.

I've already covered the first objective around self-preservation. If this was the only criterion for a Good No, you could just say no to anything unimportant to *you*, a la Bartleby the scrivener's pervasive use of "I would prefer not to."[4] Which would probably be a career-limiting and relationship-destroying way of living.

---

4 Spoiler alert. Bartleby's approach resulted with him dying of starvation. In prison. You've been warned.

The second objective balances out the first because it serves your reputation, how others perceive you, and your regard for their needs. A well-delivered Good No will not dissuade Requesters from considering you for future opportunities and collaborations. They will walk away from the interaction feeling as good about you as they did before the conversation. They might even have *more* appreciation and respect for you.

There are also emotional benefits from delivering a Good No. You may feel:
In control of your time and priorities.
Smart about how you manage expectations.
Confident in your ability to navigate difficult situations and manage relationships.
Focused on the right tasks and outcomes.
Successful at building relationships and your reputation.

So, how do you deliver a Good No? It's not a trick; it's a strategy. While it's not difficult to learn, it may take a few attempts to get it right. Most people will try to negotiate out of something by focusing on applying the right tone and combination of words that will magically set them free from commitment. Using the right tone and phrasing in reply to a request is undoubtedly a good way to sound empathetic, professional, and reasonable.

REQUESTER: *Hey, do you have some time to [insert activity or deliverable] by the end of the week?*

OVERCOMMITTED SUPERSTAR: *Oh, hey, I'd love to help. I've been wanting to get a bit more experience with this type of thing, but I'm just swamped right now.*

Not bad. But what happens when a Requester counters with a modification of the request?

REQUESTER: *That's okay. I could probably push the deadline out a few days, especially since this is something you're interested in.*

Oh great. Now the Superstar needs to come up with *another* magical sentence that explains why they can't meet the new deadline. And then perhaps another if the deadline moves out again. And then another if the Requester offers to reduce the scope. Eventually, the Superstar runs out of magic and starts repeating themselves. Or worse, they get so flustered they deliver a Bad Yes. This is essentially a tactical game that centers on phraseology instead of gaining control. Aha! Remember our toddler running around saying no and her discovery of control? We need to tap back into that "running around with peas up our noses" mindset to get control.

How do you get control? Instead of focusing on words, you must assume a ***role*** in the conversation to strengthen the foundation of your position. By role, I'm not suggesting you have to find your inner Samuel Jackson and become someone you aren't. That wouldn't work. And it would be weird. Taking on a role means communicating with specific intent and purpose. A Requester is already in a role. They are more prepared for the conversation because they initiated it. By the time they are in front of you, they have already thought about what they need and who is best suited to support that need. Once they identified you as their Superstar, they thought about how you might respond to the request based on your relationship, which then made them think about how they were going to pose the request. Requesters have the advantage of time to think about the role *they* are going to play.

Requesters can play all kinds of roles to entice and encourage you to say yes. You may recognize a few of them below.

THE FRIEND: *Hey, buddy, I need a huge favor from my favorite superstar. You're the one and only person I can trust with this. Do me a solid, huh?*

THE STARMAKER: *I have such a massive opportunity for you! It's going to get you a lot of exposure in the company and establish your personal brand.*[5]

THE MINIMIZER: *Don't worry, this isn't a big lift. You can probably knock this out in a couple of hours.*

THE HAPLESS SIMPLETON: *This type of thing is really outside my wheelhouse. I just don't know what to do. You're so good at stuff like this and it would probably take you a tenth of the time that it would take me. Can you help?*

---

5   I admit I've used this on others in the past. Not proud of it.

THE POLITICIAN: *If you can figure out a way to make this happen, I'll be sure to put in a good word for you during the next promotion cycle.*

THE DICTATOR (often someone in a position of authority): *I need you to stop everything you're doing and make this your #1 priority. Everything else goes on the back burner until I say otherwise.*

If you work with people in sales, marketing, or consulting, then you *really* have your work cut out for you because these folks get *paid* on their ability to influence people to do things they may not be able to do. They can play all sorts of roles within the same conversation and are masters at getting others to say yes.

Because Requesters are in role, *you* need to be in role. But what kind of role? We'll get into the variations in a bit. First, there are a few guiding principles to consider.

Good No Guiding Principles

Tell the truth.

This first principle may seem like a no-brainer, but we all have deployed "lies of convenience." These are the fibs we tell when someone asks us if we've ever read Dostoevsky or if we've exercised in the last week. We say yes to save ourselves embarrassment or just to maintain the flow of the conversation. And there are the slightly grayish lies we tell to get out of social activities: "Oh, I would just *love* to join you for the grand opening of the new Renaissance-themed escape room downtown, but gosh darn it, I don't think I can make it because [sniffle, cough] I might be coming down with something."[6]

The temptation to use similar tactics at work can be powerful. Resist it! Getting caught telling a white lie about a non-existent presentation you are working on for your

---

[6] No offense intended for fans of Renaissance theme parties or escape rooms.

manager that is taking up all your time could result in you taking a hit to your credibility more than it probably should. After all, a Requester could send an email to your manager asking to extend the deadline on that "presentation," which would both expose you and reflect badly on you. Don't lie.

Facilitate the conversation.

As we reviewed earlier, delivering a Good No requires more than providing a magical one-liner about why you can't do something. A Good No is a discussion, not a one-and-done response. Assume ownership of the conversation (there it is again: control) in a manner that is helpful to the Requester. How? By acknowledging that you understand the request is important to the Requester and you care about their desire to solve the problem. Spending some time exploring options and alternatives will help you come across as collaborative rather than dismissive.

Don't (over) apologize.

This principle is the toughest one to adhere to. Saying "sorry" is a handy bit of language because it can convey a broad spectrum of regret. When you're in conversation with a Requester, and you include a perfunctory "I'm sorry, I can't" as part of your Good No, you're in the safe zone. When you *over*-apologize, you open the door to being de-positioned. Take this example:

"I am so sorry, this sounds like a great assignment and I *really* wish I could help, but I have so much going on this week, and I just don't think I can swing it"

What's so bad about this? When you over-apologize like this, you suggest to the Requester that you would normally say yes to this if circumstances allowed. And in some cases, that might be true. But the Requester might also interpret this as a request for them to help free up some of your time. And herein begins the negotiation. Similar to our earlier example, a Requester may be willing to flex on the timing and say, "Hey, that's okay, I don't really need to get this done immediately. You can start on it next week when you have more time." If you have already offered a breathless apology for not being able to help without more time, the Requester could just move the due date to encourage you to commit. The lesson? By all means, be sympathetic, but don't go overboard.

To recap, tell the truth, facilitate the conversation, and avoid over-apologizing. Now, let's turn our attention to the roles.

The Roles

Remember, being "in role" does not mean you're shedding your personality and taking on a new one. You are obviously still you. A role is the position you are taking in the conversation as a means to deliver a Good No. If you focus on the position, you will find it easier to maintain control and facilitate the discussion. The *objective* for a Good No may vary. In some situations, your objective might be to remove yourself from consideration and any effort. In other situations, the goal might be to reduce the effort required to satisfy the request, especially if it falls well within the boundaries of your job description.

The following roles represent a mix of options for different scenarios. Not all of the roles and techniques will work for everyone or in every situation. Variables such as your personality and communication style, the nature of the request, and who the Requester is will influence which role might be the best fit. With practice, you will be able to quickly draw on a few of the roles in the moment when needed. Also, note that the examples here are shorter and pithier than they might be in a real-life situation to give you a general idea of what each role sounds like.

To help illustrate each of these roles, we'll visit the headquarters of BigCo, a large international company that makes, sells, and services stuff—lots of stuff—all over the world. Like most large corporations, BigCo has its mix of perks and downsides, but overall, it's a good place for someone to spend all or part of their career.

Let's head inside and bear witness to our first role: The Connector.

Connector[7]

The Connector is for those situations when you are not the best person to carry out a task. This situation pops up when a Requester is unfamiliar with the nature of your role or skill set. As a result, they make assumptions based on your job title, who your boss is, or something they heard about you from someone a few months ago.

These types of requests often receive a Bad Yes because it can be embarrassing to have to explain to someone that you don't have the capabilities or the authority the Re-

---

7   I am not blatantly ripping off Malcolm Gladwell and his absurdly successful book *The Tipping Point*, which refers to a "connector" as a person who is naturally inclined to make introductions to people that benefit everyone involved. The reference to "connector" here is describing a role, not a personality trait. I am only subtly ripping off Mr. Gladwell.

quester assumed you possessed. But it doesn't have to be that way. If you've worked at a company for even a year or two, chances are you know a lot about the responsibilities and strengths of many people inside and outside of your team. By helping the Requester find the *right* person for the task, you come across as resourceful and insightful.

When to use the Connector:

A Requester asks you to do something far outside the boundaries of your role and/or skills.

What it looks like:

Meet Pam. She's a talented project manager who has built a big fan base among her peers and the management team. It's the first week of the new year. She is at her desk, preparing a presentation for a kickoff meeting for her latest assignment.

Enter Victor. He's a newly minted vice president from another department who Pam worked with in the past on a customer service project. He's capable but still figuring out his new position. He stops by her desk. Let's go mill about and listen to their conversation.

VICTOR: *Hey, Pam. I know this request is a bit of a "blast from the past," but I need to pull all the customer service data from our call centers and dump it into a new report. Given that you did this once before on last year's project, I thought you'd be the best person to ask. You can use the same template you used before, but I'd need you to update the dates. Oh, but I would also need to pull in the data from the new call center in Costa Rica. Not sure where that is, but I bet you know how to hunt that sort of thing down. That's all. Wait, one more thing. Maybe just add a section that shows call volume by agent. Think you could you pull that together for me in the next day or so?*

Well, well. Victor isn't much for small talk, is he? But he sure knows how to make a laundry list of work feel as easy as rolling down a hill. Remember the "minimizer" approach described earlier? This is what it sounds like. Victor probably really does believe that this request isn't a big deal since Pam has already completed it once.

Pam does a quick calculation in her head. While it's true it *wouldn't* take too long to get this done, it would eat into the time she needs to prepare for her kickoff meeting. And she needs every available minute to pull all the materials together. She thinks for a bit, takes a breath, and says:

PAM: *Hey, Vic, I know exactly what you're looking for. Actually, I think the best person to do this might be Ann Adams, who runs all the analytics for that team.*

VICTOR: *Oh, okay, yeah, I've heard of her. Frankly, I think it would be easier to just have you run this.*

PAM: *I understand, but she is great to work with and she's super fast. If she'd been around last year, we would have finished our project in half the time. Let me check in with her to confirm that she still owns the reporting. If so, I'll give her a high-level overview of what you're looking for and get the two of you connected.*

Notice that last sentence. Instead of just passing the request to Ann, who may not appreciate having more work tossed on her plate without a heads-up, Pam offers to spend a bit of time to help move things forward for Victor. So, while this technique didn't remove all of Pam's effort, it significantly reduced it. And she managed to promote and endorse Ann's capabilities in the meantime.

Now, of course, it's possible that Ann may also be too busy to take on this work. In this case, Ann would have to return to Victor with her Good No. But let's set that aside for now and head down the hall to check out another example.

Educator

On the television show *Friends*, there was a running gag about how none of the characters knew what Chandler Bing did for a living.[8] If your friends and family struggle to understand what *you* do for a living, you may also experience the "Chandler effect," where you constantly have to explain your role. Sometimes to your own colleagues! Designers, consultants, engineers, marketers, anyone in corporate development and "customer success" can probably relate. These folks often get wackadoodle requests

---

8   He was responsible for "statistical analysis and data reconfiguration." Essentially, he made spreadsheets.

from people outside their team that may be directionally right but are not a match for their position or skillset.

Most of the time, this confusion is an innocent misunderstanding on the part of the Requester. But when someone feels like their coworkers don't understand what they do, it can be frustrating. And if it happens repeatedly, it can be highly annoying (in which case, you might want to talk to your boss about a title change).

The best approach is to take a breath, show some grace, and use this as an opportunity to let the Requester know what you really do.

When to use the Educator:

A Requester asks you to help with something based on a false interpretation of your role or skill set.

What it looks like:

Paul from BigCo's brand strategy team is coming out of the company cafe with his afternoon coffee. He's responsible for ensuring that the company's customers worldwide have a positive perception of the gaming division's line of video game controllers and accessories. As he passes the elevator bank, Helen from human resources pops out and spots Paul immediately. Let's stand over here and pretend to be waiting for the next elevator while we eavesdrop.

HELEN: *Hi, Paul. I was hoping I'd run into you at some point. I've been tapped to help plan the company offsite this fall. Given you're a branding guru, I thought you might be willing to lean in and help develop some logo concepts around the theme for our company offsite, 'Be Bold and Win Big.'*

PAUL: *Not sure I'd call myself a guru. My role is focused on brand strategy, not the creative stuff. We rely on our ad agency for design.*

HELEN: *Ohhhh, I didn't realize that. But your input would be super helpful for defining how to incorporate BigCo's brand into the look and feel of the logo. I've been collecting some feedback and ideas from a few of the execs and they all kind of jumble together. Think you could lend some of your big brain to the cause and help me make sense of this?*

PAUL: *I understand the challenge, believe me, and I know how important it is to get it right. I have to balance the perspectives of millions of customers every day. But this probably is less about strategy and more about getting some logo options produced quickly that you can select from. I'm not sure what your budget is, but I could send you a list of some independent designers we've worked with in the past that you could check out.*

Easy peasy, right? Helen was convinced that Paul was her answer, even though he made it clear at the beginning of the conversation that he wasn't. Notice, too, that Paul threw in a little Connector-ish offer at the end there to send Helen a list of potential people who could help her.

This was an artful way of contributing towards getting to a solution with minimal effort.

Fact Checker

If you work with colleagues who tend to inflate the urgency of their requests, the Fact Checker role can help slow things down so you can get clarity about whether you really need to clear your calendar and reprioritize all your work. Obviously, you don't want to insult the Requester by coming across as skeptical or suspicious (even if the Requester has a reputation for playing a little loose with the facts), so it's important to demonstrate interest in *understanding the problem* without committing to solving it.

When to use:

You suspect that the deadline of the request, or what is driving it, may not be completely accurate.

What it looks like:

Meet Miguel from marketing. He first came to BigCo via an internship during his senior year of college and has spent the last few years supporting campaigns for dozens of BigCo's products. He's in the break area refilling the coffee maker (what a guy).

Paula from the product team sweeps by. She's a long-time employee who has worked at multiple BigCo locations worldwide. She knows just about everyone everywhere and knows how to get things done. Paula also has a reputation for using exaggeration and borderline alarmist tactics to move her requests to the top of everyone's to-do list. But she gets results and, because of that, BigCo executives love her. Seeing Miguel, she alters course and zips into the break area.

Let's pretend to look for some granola bars while we listen, shall we?

PAULA: Oh my gosh, Miguel! How ARE you? You have been on my mind all morning. The Condor product team just got some big news. Now it's not official, and you absolutely cannot share this with anyone, but we are very, very close to getting our biggest distributor to co-sponsor our launch campaign. They are going all-in and are willing to pony up budget and people, and even feature the product in their own marketing materials. We've never had this much interest and support from a distributor before. I mean this is HUGE. We're probably going to have to have our entire product leadership clear their calendars and make this their number-one priority. To get this going, I think we'll likely need a three-day joint work session with the distributor team to get all the pieces in place. The customer wants this too. Everyone on the extended team agrees that you're the best person to pull together the materials. And I TOTALLY agree. You are the best. When can you get this started?"

Let's hit the pause button for a second and give our ears a break while Paula inhales. Are you picking up some signals that the facts are a bit, shall we say, "elastic" on Planet Paula? She mentioned that this news is "not official." The leadership team is "probably" going to have to "clear their calendars." And she "thinks" they will "likely need" to run a multi-day workshop. Of course, it's possible that this plan may in fact be rubber-stamped already. Or it will be. But maybe it won't be. This could all be wishful thinking.

Let's see how Miguel handles this.

MIGUEL: Wow, thanks for thinking of me, Paula. Before I commit to this, I'm curious to know a bit more from you, the extended team, and the folks you've been meeting with on the customer side. I want to make sure I understand the needs and expectations of everyone involved. Do you have a check-in scheduled with the team I can join to learn more?

Oooh, nice. Notice how Miguel demonstrated curiosity about the request without coming across as suspicious. There's a bit of nuance at play here. As we saw in the exchange between Victor and Pam, Miguel offered to do *some* work by asking to be included in a team meeting. This isn't exactly a clean break. Miguel is only committing to a conversation, not a huge workstream. For now, anyway.

Taking on the Fact Checker role also helps Miguel get a read on how legit this request is in real-time. If no meetings are scheduled, then the onus is on Paula to do a little more work to get things set up before Miguel has to drop everything he's doing.

If a check-in meeting is scheduled, that's good, too. Miguel has created space and time to gather more context about the agreed-upon outcomes and confirm that the team really wanted him to put the workshop materials together.

Paula might be interpreting his response as "Oh, I am SOOO in, sign me up!" That's okay. After Miguel has collected the facts (from attending the check-in), he will know whether this work should fall to him based on availability, capability, and role. Either way, he will have to make a decision and communicate it back to Paula. Coming out of a fact-checking activity and going back to the Requester without a firm commitment to do something or not do something (with a suitable reason) can come across as wishy-washy and may hurt one's credibility.

Let's suppose that Miguel's instincts were right, and the facts don't support his participation. Maybe the extended team mentioned Miguel's name as someone who might have ideas but not the person to own the work, and Paula just got carried away in the moment. Or maybe the distributor doesn't, in fact, want the workshop. Or perhaps the types of materials needed aren't something Miguel has access to. If any of these are true, Miguel will need to use the data he's collected to explain to Paula why he will not be taking on the assignment.

Translator

Requesters don't always know how to describe the outcome they're looking for or the type of work they need someone to perform. They may ask for much more than they really need to to ensure they don't end up with less. Or they may load up on vague, nonsensical corporate-speak to make it sound like they are bringing an earnest, important, well-defined request to the table.

The Translator's goal is to interpret the request as best they can and communicate a more precise and accurate description of the outcome and effort. Being a good Translator is like being on a cooking reality show where contestants are given a random bunch of ingredients to build a delicious meal. Translators also have to work with a list of random ingredients. They need to take a shopping cart of disconnected objectives, activities, and ideas and create a piping-hot dish of sense. If you're a good listener and puzzler who can quickly put ideas together on the fly, then you're a natural Translator.

When to use:

The request is unclear, non-specific, or unrealistic, but it is in your domain of expertise.

What it looks like:

Let's go down a couple of floors to meet Devon, a developer who works on BigCo's web pages in North America. He's got his big headphones clamped to his head and looks like he's got a groove going on as he bops his head to the beat while he bangs out some code. Over his shoulder, we can see Dan from the digital experience team coming this way. Dan isn't Devon's boss, but he's on the team that develops the strategy around making BigCo customers happy, so there is a slight overlap between their worlds. Dan is waving his hand in front of Devon's face to get his attention. Yeesh. Let's hide behind this big old monitor no one's using and see what's up.

DAN: *My guy! Sorry to interrupt you, but I am desperate for some help. I'm working on this 'rapid-path-to-fulfillment-journey' thing for all our small business customers to create a better glide path to purchase. It's super slick, but I need to concretize the thinking into a mock-up that I can show the higher-ups to get buy-in. I'm thinking of something like an omni-track digital flow, where every product has a dedicated website experience that highlights key feature sets based on the customer's firmographic profile, which eventually dumps them back into a headless commerce model. I would love to pick your brain[9] and get some medium-high fidelity concepts put together that I can shop around.*

Um. What?

Let's give Devon's brain a moment to digest that bowl of semantic stew and translate it from *corporate-ese* to English. In the meantime, let's review that bit about brain-picking and ideas to shop around. While Dan's goal may be just to

---

9 Gross, by the way. Don't ever say this.

get some quick perspective and move on, "ideas" can be a Trojan horse for a much bigger request. It comes down to packaging. An idea can be anything from a thought expressed in a couple of sentences to a fully blown-out presentation with slides, images, and prototypes. People with jobs like Devon's, requiring deeper design and creativity capabilities, often feel pushed to go into "execution mode" because they're good at making things look good.

Let's check back in on Devon.

DEVON: *I'm hearing you say that, ultimately, the goal is to help small business customers make a purchase decision faster. Is that correct?*

DAN: *Basically, yeah.*

DEVON: *Got it. Well. If you want to get something up and running quickly, I would suggest creating ONE menu of the three main product groups on a single page. The customer can click on the group they want to get to a list of the individual products. It's a more traditional design, but it will get customers to the right product in two clicks and reduce the likelihood that they'll get lost on our site. And it's easy to update when you want to add more products.*

DAN: *That's true. Is that something you can build out?*

DEVON: *Our team can turn around a new page in a few days. But it sounds like you just need a visual to show the leadership team. I can pull together a mock-up of what those two pages might look like that you can use for the presentation. It won't take long, but I do have a few other things I need to finish up first. I'll send you something by end of day tomorrow. Once you get it approved by leadership, then we can schedule the actual build-out.*

Devon did two bits of translating here. First, he interpreted and rearticulated the outcome Devon sought ("a web page"). Once that was clear, he broke down the scope and timing for the "packaging" of the ideas. Actually, he did something better. Devon defined *for Dan* what the deliverable would look like and when it would be ready based on *Devon's* timetable.

Deferrer

Some people are prone to delivering a Bad Yes due to temporary stress-induced acquiescence.[10] Stress from decision-making under pressure can be incredibly taxing. When the brain gets overwhelmed with decisions because Requesters are looking for an immediate response, it signals to the rest of the body, "This doesn't feel good. Get us outta here!" And ironically, the quickest way out is a Bad Yes. Goodbye, "decision-making-stress." Hello, "I-don't-have-time-to-get-all-this-shit-done stress!"

But with the luxury of time to consider options, someone might arrive at a different answer. The Deferrer role focuses on creating space to consult with others, explore alternatives, or just review your calendar. When assuming

---

10 Not a real medical condition.

the Deferrer role, it's important to let the Requester know how long it will take to respond.

When to use:

You aren't in the right mindset to make an informed decision about how or if you can help.

What it looks like:

Let's go across BigCo's campus and drop in on Sherry, who is on the services delivery team. She works on consulting projects that BigCo sells to its largest customers. She is always spread across two or three customers and is mindful of where she spends her time because her client hours are billable. In fact, here she is entering her hours for the week when the head of consulting sales, Cybil, sidles up. Let's ease up on our pace as we walk by so we can get the skinny.

CYBIL: *Sherry! How goes it with BigCo's biggest secret weapon in services? Listen. We have a quick-turn proposal that needs to get out the door by the end of the week. The scope is identical to the project you just started. Would be great to get your eyes and brain on this.*

SHERRY: *Hi, Cybil. Wow, that is a tight timeline. I have quite a few things in motion right now, and my manager is asking me to sit in on some applicant interviews for positions on our team. Let me talk to her and I will get back to you in twenty-four hours.*

Solid. No notes. A caution, though. The Deferrer role is the one that is most prone to telling little white or gray lies about competing priorities that don't exist. Let's say Sherry's line about helping out with applicant interviews wasn't true. Cybil could go to Sherry's manager and ask her to free her up from hiring activities so she could work on the proposal, which would lead to confusion and awkwardness, and reflect badly on Sherry.

Resist the temptation. Remember, *tell the truth*. If you need time to consider your options but don't have a competing activity you can name off the top of your head, just ask for time to look at your schedule and be clear about when you will get back to the Requester.

Scope Artist

Requesters may arrive bearing a task that they don't have the skills or the experience to handle with a fantastical estimate of how long it should take to complete. Designers, data analysts, and anyone with specialized skills often find themselves in these scenarios over their careers. Why do generalists think they know better than the specialists how much effort it takes to do their job?[11]

The Scope Artist role is worth adopting if you are a specialist with a good eye and head for guesstimating. It requires having enough experience delivering the goods on time, every time to give your response credibility and

---

11 I am a generalist, and I approve this message.

weight. If you're new to your specialty or your job, or if the request is for a task you don't have much experience with, your response may trigger a more drawn-out debate.

When to use:

The Requester is grossly underestimating how long a request will take to complete.

What it looks like:

Let's head down to the hallowed hallways that house the data science team to meet Darryl, a master of mathematical gymnastics. He's responsible for digging into BigCo's data to generate reports, insights, and strategy "ahas" to help guide business decisions. Lucky for us, he keeps his work area lit low to reduce eyestrain, so let's just slide back into the corner here as Sam from sales operations approaches.

SAM: *Hey, Darryl, you probably saw those two spreadsheets I sent you a few minutes ago. I figured it would be easier to talk you through what I need rather than put it in an email. I'm trying to get clear on the average amount customers in Australia spent with us and a new company we bought last year versus this year. I've got all the purchase orders I need on the two spreadsheets but I can't get the account names or the numbers to line up because it all came from two different databases. Can you scrub the data, merge everything together, and put in some filters so I can look up totals by account, location, and products? For a numbers guy like you, this is kid's stuff, I bet. Probably take less than an hour.*

Darryl: *I took a look at the spreadsheets. You're right, there are quite a few discrepancies between them. I had to do something similar last month for the Canadian market. Some of this is just routine clean-up that I can knock out in fifteen minutes, but to get it completely scrubbed is going to require some manual effort that will take the better part of two days to finish. I can't free up that much time on short notice, but I can add this to the queue and start working on it by the end of next week. Does that work for you?*

Lots to like here. First, Darryl did a good job credentialing himself right away by referencing similar work he has done in the past before getting into his assessment of what needs to get done, when the work can begin, and how long it will take. At this point, Sam has to make a decision. Does he want to accept Darryl's timeline and move forward with someone who is very likely to deliver the outcome he wants? Or does he want to spend more time trying to find someone who might be able to deliver something faster but perhaps not with the same level of quality?

Metrics Magician

In order to survive and thrive, a healthy business needs to measure how stuff gets developed and sold, and how it performs. Rightly or wrongly, business adages like "what gets measured, gets managed"[12] and "show me a company's metrics, and I'll show you their culture"[13] are proven true when employees and leaders prioritize activities that directly impact their ability to get paid and promoted. High performers quickly learn that the bigger your job, the more metrics you own. While a metric-centric mindset has merits and disadvantages, it creates conflict when Requesters push for something that only benefits them, not the person being asked (who has their own set of performance metrics). Saying no to a Requester who is at risk of missing their goals, disappointing their boss, and impacting their career is hard. But not as hard as when you say yes and put yourself at risk of missing *your* goals, disappointing *your* boss, and impacting *your* career.

When to use:

The request inhibits your ability to achieve measurable milestones that are an expectation of your role.

---

[12] Often misattributed to Peter Drucker and almost always misinterpreted as words to lead by. The full quote from V.F. Ridgway's 1956 paper, *Dysfunctional Consequences of Performance Measurements*, reads, "What gets measured gets managed — even when it's pointless to measure and manage it, and even if it harms the purpose of the organisation to do so."

[13] Many people have claimed credit for a version of this gem. This one's mine.

What it looks like:

BigCo is so big and has so much data about markets, customers, and industries that the company created an entire division dedicated to researching and creating tailored reports for its most valuable customers. Let's take a stroll over to check out what Ingrid from the industries team is working on. Looks like she's about to have a little confab with Siobhan from sales, who's been having a rough year.

SIOBHAN: *Ingrid. Really need your help. I have a customer that is a huge pain in the ass, pardonnez mon Francais. They keep threatening to go to another provider because they say we're too transactional and not showing them that we really understand their business. They're not the biggest spenders, but I can't afford to lose them right now because it will work against my quota. I kind of told them we could maybe give them some market research tailored just for them…pro bono. I know I shouldn't have promised anything without talking to you first, but I've got my back against the wall here. I can't lose them this late in the year without slipping below quota. Do you have some cycles you can free up to give them something to keep them off my back?*

INGRID: *Ouch. I hear you. As you said, it's the end of the year, and I also have to make sure I am hitting my goals. If I don't prioritize clients who are paying for these reports, then I run the risk of missing my targets. And right now, I need to spend my time making sure that I'm on track. If I free up in the next few days, I will let you know, but right now, I have to focus on what's in front of me."*

This example is probably the most direct we've come across so far. But that's okay. Being direct when talking about competing performance goals is often best because it acknowledges the pressure each person is under and the similarity of what's causing it. Notice that Ingrid didn't mention Siobhan's misstep of overpromising pro bono work. That would have been argumentative, and frankly, making Siobhan feel guilty would not have helped. By focusing on the topic that both of them could relate to ("metrics"), Ingrid kept the conversation from going into a less helpful, emotionally charged direction.

Arbitrator

Occasionally, a Good No may be required to manage expectations from a Good Yes. Sometimes, someone agrees to a request that is appropriate, reasonable, and executable within an agreed-upon time limit and then, *dun-dun-dun-DAAAH*, the Requester comes back with additional needs, changes, or new directions without altering expectations around timing.

When this happens, there are two options. Be the hero everyone says you are and roll with the changes, especially if the work is a core part of your role. But if you start to feel like you're overcommitting, then the second option is to become your own arbitrator and reset the terms with the Requester.

When to use:

Your Requester keeps "moving the goalposts" and asks for more scope than you can reasonably deliver within the agreed-upon timeframe.

What it looks like:

Let's stroll over to the far corner of BigCo, where Camelia from corporate communications sits. Most of her work focuses on ensuring employees and customers are always up to speed on how BigCo's strategies may affect them and their lives. Recently, she agreed to help out Ian from investor relations, who is responsible for keeping BigCo's shareholders informed about anything that may affect the price of their stock. We'll pretend to admire the corporate wall art hanging in the corridor while we listen in.

IAN: *What you've done here so far is really good. Better than I could have done by myself, that's for sure. I think we are very close to the finish line. I have a few ideas I'd like you to play with and then there are a couple of sections I want to add to the top. I included my notes in the document, but let me know if you have any questions while you're working on the next draft.*

CAMELIA: *I'm glad you're feeling good about where things are. As I said during our first conversation, I was more than happy to get an initial rough draft pushed out and then toss it back to you for revisions going forward. I've done two drafts within the timeframe we agreed to, but I'm now at a point where I really need to get caught up on the things I pushed to the side so I could help you. I'm sure you understand.*

As we've seen in other exchanges with BigCo folks, Camelia stuck to the facts and limited her talking points to the agreed-upon deliverables. It would be hard for Ian to counter (though he might try) with a follow-on request requiring Camelia to take more time away from her other work.

But let's suppose the Requester in this example wasn't someone from another team, but Camelia's boss. Or someone she doesn't report to but who still has a higher level of authority in the business. Pushing back against scope creep from a higher-up might not work too well. For those situations, there is another role to consider…

The Recruiter

Delivering a Good No to a manager or a superior can be daunting. Especially for those who work in a hierarchical, political, do-as-I-say culture. Remember the earlier example of "the dictator" role Requesters sometimes play? In these situations, delivering a Good No feels so risky it might as well be a "Good-bye." But for some people, it can be difficult to say no even to the warmest, jolliest Bambi-like boss within the cuddliest of company cultures.

In business, everyone has a boss. Even the CEO or owner of the company is accountable to someone: customers, the board of directors, investors, analysts, suppliers, union leaders, or regulators. Everyone has expectations placed on them that are measured and monitored. The higher up in the food chain you are, the greater the expectation.[14] The further away a Requester is from hitting their financial target, quota, or deadline, the more urgent the request and, thus, the higher the stakes for the person receiving the request.

The Arbitrator role presented earlier exercises a type of *positional* negotiating where the Good No strategy is rooted in fact and logic to bring someone around to one's way of thinking. Higher-stakes conversations involving more formidable stakeholders on the other side require *interest-based* negotiating that focuses on creating a mutual win for both parties. The Recruiter takes advantage of the authority and influence the Requester has to change the rules, shift resources, or reprioritize the work of others in order to create a win-win.

When to use:

The Requester is someone with influence and authority who you should really say yes to, but you need the conditions to be improved.

---

14   I worked with a CEO of a Fortune 500 company who liked to remind people, "I only make three or four decisions a year. But they are BIG decisions."

What it looks like:

If we cut across the BigCo cafeteria, we can catch up with Paula from the publicity team, who is about to be intercepted by her boss's boss, Charlie, the chief marketing officer. Charlie has only been at BigCo for a couple of months. Paula has been in a few meetings with him but doesn't know him all that well. She's heard from others on her team that he works very hard to make an impression on the executive committee but can be a bit gruff when he's stressed. And he's always stressed. Let's slow our pace so we can hear what's driving his latest wave of anxiety.

CHARLIE: *Paula! Been looking for you. I have a board meeting next week, and I'd like to share a summary of the publicity campaigns we ran over the last three months. Most of the presentations are going to be slides, but I'd like to do something a bit flashier. I'm thinking we should use video to bring a little excitement into the room. I'm going to be neck-deep in prep sessions all weekend, so I'll need it by mid-day Friday. Okay?*

PAULA: *Wow! That's great you want to feature the campaigns. I think video would be a great way to energize the meeting.*

CHARLIE: *Great, let me know when you have a rough cut so I can provide feedback.*

PAULA: *Absolutely, Charlie. Just so you know, I've been 100% dedicated to our college recruitment campaign materials, which are due to the human resources team next week.*

CHARLIE: *I think that can wait. The board should take precedence.*

PAULA: *Of course. I understand. Would it be okay if I send them a note letting them know that I need to push the deliverable back a few days and CC you? Then you can respond to everyone with an email letting them know the need to prioritize the board meeting.*

CHARLIE: *You don't need to CC me. They'll understand.*

PAULA: *I'm sure they will, but their SVP, Haley, has been the one setting the deadlines, and we've already had some delays. It would help to have some air cover.*

CHARLIE: *I get it. That's fine. CC me and I'll come over the top with a follow-up. If you get pushback from anyone else, let me know."*

Aw, didn't that scene trigger the warm and fuzzies for you? Yeah, me neither. But notice how Paula was able to apply some Good No jiujitsu and turn the weight of Charlie's authority into an asset by recruiting him to provide air cover for her so she can reprioritize her efforts and get Charlie his deliverable without the fear of receiving blowback from another executive.

There is another scenario where the Recruiter role can be helpful: stretch assignments. Saying yes to stretch assignments is almost always the correct answer for someone who is trying to grow professionally. But because they usually involve developing new skills, additional scope, and/or unfamiliar topic areas, a "conditional yes"[15] may be needed to set yourself up for success.

Let's say Paula's calendar wasn't all that full. And Charlie's request was not about the board meeting. Instead, let's say he wanted Paula to take the lead on a marketing analytics project, even though Paula doesn't have any analytics in her background, though she *does* have lots of experience as a people manager.

In this instance, Paula might say something like, "Thank you for this opportunity, and I'd very much like to take this on. Given this would be a new area for me, I have some specific people in mind with strong analytic skills that I'd like to have on the team. Would you be open to helping me bring some of them on to the project?" This response doesn't *feel* aggressively conditional, but it does convey what Paula needs to be successful and how Charlie can use his authority to provide a reasonable amount of resources to support her.

The Vanquished

You may have moments when you are legitimately utterly incapable of taking on any request, no matter how urgent. Your calendar is a big black box of meetings.

---

15 I'm being descriptive here. I definitely would not recommend responding to a stretch assignment request with the words "only on condition."

There is a family member or friend that needs your attention. You're sick and can't afford to "play hurt."[16] You don't need to take on anything else because you're not a superhero, and you're not Florence flipping Nightingale. In those situations, you have to appeal to the humanity of the Requester, wave the white flag, and tap out.

When to use:

When you absolutely and positively cannot take on one more thing without doing damage to yourself.

What it looks like:

Our time at BigCo is coming to an end, and we need to drop off our visitor badges at the security desk. Looks like Sean, who is managing the desk, isn't doing too well. He seems a little distracted by a text thread on his phone. He has a furrowed brow and a concerned look on his face. His boss, Cheryl, is coming over to him. Let's take our time turning in these badges so we can listen in.

CHERYL: *Sean, we're down a couple of folks for the weekend night shifts. Can I count on you to take on the Saturday shift?*

SEAN: *I can't this weekend.*

CHERYL: *Sean, you're the one always asking to pick up some overtime. And we are* really *short. I need you.*

---

[16] Classic bro-culture term. And so stupid. You know what happens when you "play hurt?" You stay hurt.

SEAN: *Cheryl, I appreciate the offer. And I am interested in overtime, but I have a family matter that I need to take care of this weekend. I hope you understand and will keep me in mind for extra shifts in the future.*

The Vanquished role is magical because it almost always relieves you from unneeded obligations. And for that reason, it should be applied sparingly and only when the conditions warrant. You don't want to develop a reputation as the perpetual hot mess in the office who is always hanging off the edge of the abyss by their pinky toe. So make sure when you DO use the Vanquished role, you're speaking the truth about your current state. You don't have to share details about what's going on with you. Keep it high level, be clear that it is non-negotiable, and leave it at that.

One more thing. If you find yourself in a Vanquished state on a regular basis *because of* work, or your Requesters are unsympathetic to your plight and insist that you take on the task, you may want to take a step back and think about making some changes in your work world to preserve your physical and mental health.

How Am I Supposed to Remember All These Dang Roles?

You're not. And you shouldn't. It's unrealistic to expect that anyone could summon up a mental menu of roles while in conversation with a Requester and scroll to the right one for the occasion. Also, there are roles that may not gel with your personality or communication style. As you were reading through the descriptions of the roles, there were probably more than a few where you thought, "That's not me, I would never do this." While (hopefully) for other roles, you were thinking, "Oh I am *so* going to be using that in the future." If you can find one or two roles to keep in your back pocket, or even a combo version that suits you, that's probably enough to help you manage your next few Good No conversations when the occasion calls for it.

To identify the best role for you, think back to the last time you responded to a Requester with a Bad Yes. What was the nature of the request? How was it presented to you? What was the demeanor and personality of the Requester? If you could go back in time with the knowledge of the roles, which one would have worked best in that circumstance?[17] Now think back to another Bad Yes moment, ideally with a different Requester. Would the same role you picked in the first Bad Yes redo have worked as well in the second? If so, then that might be the best role to put in play the next time you need to deliver a Good No.

Start with one or two roles that are the best fit for the types of requests you receive and play around with them. Over time, you'll find yourself pulling from a combo platter of roles to get and maintain control naturally and easily.

---

17 "Best" meaning which role would have suited your communication style and successfully relieved you of making a unwanted commitment while maintaining your relationship and reputation with the Requester.

Bullies, Bias, and Bullshit

All the roles in this book were created with the assumption that your Requesters are reasonable, respectful, and equitable human beings. But, of course, that's not always the case. Not everyone is well-meaning. Not everyone is polite. Some people are toxic assholes. You can choose to ignore them, forgive them, and convince yourself that they are good people deep down. But that doesn't make them any less miserable to interact with. And if those toxic personality types are in a position of authority, they may feel empowered to unleash their nihilistic, narcissistic, sociopathic side with abandon. They may use everything from wormy passive-aggressiveness to abusive, even bias-led, behavior to get what they want from the people who work for them. How does one deliver a Good No to someone like that?

You don't.

Good Nos only work when dealing with people who are essentially "good." When unreasonable and unrelenting demands hail down from the not-so-good Requesters, none of the roles will help you. Even the Vanquished role may be met with cold indifference. In those situations, other measures need to be taken to change your working conditions. You must lean into people who can help make that happen, including your boss,[18] your boss's boss, your union steward, your coach, or a human resources representative. Ask if you can move to a different team or a different manager. If you're fortunate enough to work for a company that offers counseling and mental health services, or if your insurance will cover those services, you should take full advantage of them. None of these conversations are easy. But they'll be easier to have than the conversations you aren't able to have with a toxic Requester. So be sure to lean into the people outside of work who you can count on to treat you with respect, kindness, and, yeah, love.

If you can't change the working conditions within your current company, then you really need to consider changing employers. Also not a simple solution, especially in a tough job market, but the alternative is unacceptable. Remaining in an environment where you are continually feeling unfulfilled, stressed, and insecure will impact your mental and physical health. Work can be hard. That's why it's called "work." But it shouldn't hurt you.

---

18 Assuming, of course, your boss isn't the toxic Requester you are trying to escape from.

How Much Time Do You Have Anyway

High performers often find themselves up against one of the toughest, most formidable, unforgiving Requesters in the world: themselves. New tasks pop up every day. Instead of asking for help or delegating to others, your brain thinks, "I'll just do it." Why? Because in the moment, when you have a long list of things that need to get done, it feels easier to just *do* the new thing yourself rather than spend time finding someone else who *could* do the thing, which would require taking more time to explain the thing to be done.

Oh, ye self-Requesters, No thyself!

The best way to avoid Bad Yes scenarios is to get a handle on how much time you actually have in your life. If someone asked you how long it takes you to get ready in the morning, chances are you'd give an answer that hits pretty close to the median. The time it takes to complete repetitive, routinized activities is pretty easy to calculate.

Especially when those activities are sandwiched between a known start and stop point such as the time you usually wake up and when you start work.

But estimating the time to complete "novel" tasks with open parameters is a bit harder. When we are doing work that requires deeper thinking, analysis, pattern recognition, or creativity, it's difficult to estimate how long it will take us to get to a satisfactory outcome. We fall victim to the "planning fallacy,"[19] which posits that we are likely to underestimate the time it takes for us to complete our own tasks.

Let's say you are a researcher for a packaged food company that wants to get into the oatmeal business. You have been tasked with some light deskwork to develop a two to three page summary of the oatmeal market and a couple of rough concepts for new oatmeal-like products. You know that, at a minimum, you will need to gather some data from the internet, summarize it, generate some ideas, and package it up. How long would it take? An hour? Two? An afternoon? A week?

Whatever your answer, you would probably be wrong. It would likely take longer.

---

19 Proposed by Daniel Kahneman and Amos Tversky in their research report, "Intuitive prediction: Biases and corrective procedures," 1979.

"He who every morning plans the transactions of that day and follows that plan carries a thread that will guide him through the labyrinth of the most busy life."
– Victor Hugo

Ol' Vic was on to something. To manage your time, you must first be able to account for it. And the best way to account for it is to use a tool you likely refer to dozens of times a day: your calendar. Most people use their calendars to schedule events and to-do lists to track the work they need to do. The problem with this system is they assume that enough time exists between all the events and meetings to get the work done.

Some people block off a few hours here and there for "head-down time" dedicated to checking off items on the to-do list. While this is a good practice, an even better one is transferring each item on the to-do list to the calendar as if it were an event and allot the estimated time it will take to complete. You might just need a two-hour block one morning, or a dozen thirty-minute blocks over a month. The purpose is to "balance the books" between the effort you have to spend and the time you can afford to dedicate (while being mindful of all the other priorities in your life). If you underestimate the time it takes, or if an unforeseen conflict comes up, reschedule the activity as you would a meeting or a lunch date. Scheduling time with yourself is the only way to know how much of yourself is left over to take on something more.

Summary

I hope the roles and techniques shared in this book are relevant, actionable, and helpful to you and your future negotiations with the Requesters in your life. May you find your future self feeling more in command of your time and energy as you reach ever higher levels of fulfillment and fortune.

Remember…

Usually, the correct answer is yes. But not always.

Tell the truth. Facilitate the conversation. Don't over-apologize.

Start with one or two roles that best fit your personality, communication style, and workplace.

Beware of falling into the perpetual Vanquished role. But if you do, ask for help.

Schedule your work instead of creating to-do lists.

Good luck and goodbye.

Acknowledgments

I would not have written this book without the following people's encouragement, guidance, badgering, and support. (It works out to about one person per every three or four pages, so feel free to claim credit for whatever section you want). Thank you!

Vivianne Castillo
Brad Cummings
Em Daigle
Drew Davidson
Jonathan Dien
Nic Dimond
Erica Ellis
Marc Escobosa
Elizabeth Glenewinkel

Ann Hintzman
Laura Hyde Page
Kelly Lewis
Kyrsten Musich
Shailesh Patel
Clay Stelzer
Beth Warren
Teddy Zmrhal

www.ingramcontent.com/pod-product-compliance
Lightning Source LLC
Chambersburg PA
CBHW052034030426
42337CB00027B/4995